# Golib Kholjigitov

# Finance for kids with Dino

Golib Kholjigitov

# Finance for kids with Dino

## A unique step-by-step visual guide to improve financial literacy

JustFiction Edition

**Imprint**
Any brand names and product names mentioned in this book are subject to trademark, brand or patent protection and are trademarks or registered trademarks of their respective holders. The use of brand names, product names, common names, trade names, product descriptions etc. even without a particular marking in this work is in no way to be construed to mean that such names may be regarded as unrestricted in respect of trademark and brand protection legislation and could thus be used by anyone.

Cover image: www.ingimage.com

Publisher:
JustFiction! Edition
is a trademark of
Dodo Books Indian Ocean Ltd., member of the OmniScriptum S.R.L Publishing group
str. A.Russo 15, of. 61, Chisinau-2068, Republic of Moldova Europe
Printed at: see last page
ISBN: 978-3-659-47045-5

Rawr! Hi kiddo!

Understanding money, is very important for your future. To be financially successful, you must work hard and make sure you balance your saving and spending habits.

Dino is a dinosaur who knows a lot about the science of money. He has a Ph.D. degree in Financial Power from the University of Money.

In this book Dino will help you understand how to use money, make investments and most importantly - have enough cash on hand to buy more toys. Follow Dino to discover the secrets of finance!

# What is money?

Money is a special ticket that helps pay for anything. So, if you want to buy games, food or things for the home you need money!

Remember that each item has its own unique price and it is called **value**.

Dino uses the currency called - "Dinar" to buy fruits, toys and games and other things he enjoys.

# The value of money

1 apple costs 2 Dinars.
When Dino wants to buy 1 apple,
he must pay 2 Dinars.

1 apple = 2 Dinars

The value of money is the quantity of apples that can be exchanged for it. The amount of apples that can be bought with dinars is also known as purchasing power.

| 2 apples | = | 4 Dinars |
|---|---|---|
| 3 apples | = | 6 Dinars |

# Appreciation and Depreciation

The value of money, depends on the changing prices.  If the price for an apple changes, so will the amount of apples you can buy.

When the prices rise, Dino can buy less apples. This is called a depreciation.

When the prices fall, Dino can buy more apples. This is called an appreciation.

# Example:

For example, Dino has 4 Dinars. How many apples can he buy?

| Depreciation | Appreciation |
| --- | --- |
| If the price for 1 apple rises to 3 Dinars | If the price for 1 apple falls to 1 Dinar |
| Dino can buy 1 apple | Dino can buy 4 apples |

Remember that Dino has 4 Dinars. Now how many apples can Dino buy if:

| | |
| --- | --- |
| 1 apple costs 4 Dinars | 1 apple costs 2 Dinars |
| 1 apple costs 5 Dinars | 1 apple costs 1 Dinar |

# Main properties of money

1. **Means of exchange:** Dino can use money in exchange for apples and bananas. This is more convenient than exchanging apples for bananas.

2. **Store of value:** Dino doesn't have to buy all the apples and bananas today, he can buy them as needed and save and the rest.

# Value and income

**1.** Value is created when money is invested and when 1 Dinar becomes more than 1 Dinar. For example, if 1 banana costs 4 Dinars and sold for 6 Dinars, a profit of 50% has been made and value is created [(6-4)/4] = 50%.

Dino bought 1 banana for 4 Dinars

Then Dino sold it for 6 Dinars

Profit

**2.** Income is money that you get for completing tasks or chores. People can also get income from dividends (money paid to investors from company's profits). So, Dino can have more than one source of income:

Pocket money

Money for completing chores

Dividends or interest paid by bank

# Concepts on Saving and Investing

1. **Time Value of Money** assumes a dollar in the present is worth more than a dollar in the future because of inflation and interest rates, as well as <u>opportunity cost.</u> **Opportunity cost** is the loss of the benefit that could have been received if the best investment option was chosen.

*For example: 100 Dinars today is worth more than 100 Dinars in 5 years (if not invested).*

**Example of opportunity cost:** today Dino sold one apple for 2 Dinars. If tomorrow price of apple increased to 3 Dinars, his potential loss (opportunity cost) is 1 Dinar.

If today apple costs 2 Dinars and income after selling it at price of 2 Dinars will be zero.

If tomorrow apple price increases to 3 Dinars, Dino's potential income (opportunity cost) will be 1 Dinar

# Concepts on Saving and Investing (continued)

2. **Interest** is the money that bank pays to its savers for investing (keeping) their money in a bank. Interest is given as a percentage (%), and there are two types, simple and compound (explained later).

Usually Dino keeps his money in the bank. In return bank gives Dino some extra money, which is called an interest.

Dino gives bank his 100 Dinars for 1 year at the interest rate of 10%. In 1 year Dino will get 110 Dinars from the bank (100 Dinars is principle; and 10 Dinar is interest income).

Now tell Dino, how much return would he get if he puts 100 Dinars in the Dino bank with the following interest rates:

20%

30%

# Concepts on Saving and Investing (continued)

3. **Inflation** happens when prices rise due to increases in production costs or when there is more money chasing the same amount of products produced in the country.

Today apple costs
2 Dinars

In a year it costs
4 Dinars

In the above instance, apple production quantity is fixed at 1000 units

4. **Assets** - are the items that generate money.
*Financial assets include stocks and bonds.*
*Real assets include houses and equipment.*

# Concepts on Saving and Investing (continued)

**4.Taxes** – are the Dinars that governments take from people and  businesses **to pay for public services** such as public schools, hospitals, roads and police.

Ask your parents what kind of taxes they pay?

What is the maximum income tax rate in your country?

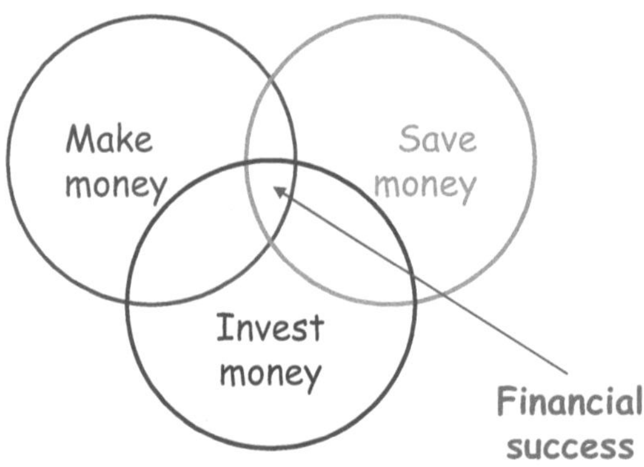

# Saving and Spending

If Dino spends more than he earns, he will borrow and have to pay back that money with interest. Too much of borrowing may lead him to loose his toys and games. To avoid this, Dino should know  the following:

EARNING — is the ability to make money by working

SPENDING — is the ability to spend wisely

SAVING — is the ability to use less money than you earn

# Budget and planning

**1. Know your income and expenses.**

Expenses

- Taxes
- Rent
- Food
- Transport

Income

- Salary
- Investments

Dino should earn more money **than he spends, and plan his expenses.** With this, he can have extra money to buy more toys or games in the future.

# Budget

## 2. **Create a personal budget plan.**

There are many approaches to create a budget. One of them is "The 70/30 rule!" 70% of income is spent on important things and 30% of income is saved.

Try to find the best prices for fixed expenses such as rent: **search and compare options before buying them.**

Now, Dino wants you to develop a budget based on your lowest possible income. Don't forget "The 70/30" rule! Further down the text we will demonstrate another budget approach using "The 50-20-30" rule.

3. **Find a method to track your budget.** Knowing where you spend your money will help to control them.

4. **Have a mindful spending** –  this is a happy way to save and maintain financial freedom. It's all about choices!

# Practice budget:

Now Dino wants to know what will you buy if you have pocket money of 100 Dinars?

 Apple costs 2 Dinars

 Banana costs 2 Dinars

 Candy costs 4 Dinars

 Cap costs 5 Dinars

 Shoes cost 12 Dinars

 Ball costs 10 Dinars

 Smartphone costs 35 Dinars

 Notebook costs 55 Dinars

 Bicycle costs 65 Dinars

Remember the 70/30 rule! 70% of income spent on important expenses and 30% put into savings.

# Spending

1. **Money is limited**, so keep monitoring your expenses. Try not to borrow too much.

2. **Know to count** and use your money wisely.

3. **Have a budget** – plan revenue and expenses and live within your means. Ask yourself 3 questions before buying something:

Do I need it?

Do I need it now?

What will happen, if I don't have it?

# Borrowing

1. If you borrow, **pay in time and in full!**

2. **Pause before spending** to consider how you feel about the purchases of toys and games.

3. **Spend wisely** and live a happy life!

# Smart Spending

<u>Before spending money Dino usually does the following:</u>

1. Takes a pause

2. Takes three deep breaths

3. Thinks about how this spending may affect his life

4. Considers whether it is something to live without

 # Saving and Investment

1. One of the most important things you should know about money, is the "**time value of money**" concept.

Time value of money means that unused (not smartly invested) money now, is worth less in the future.

Why? This happens because of a missed investment opportunities or inflation. Therefore, you should use them by investing wisely.

100 Dinars will not be worth much in 20 years, if they are hidden in a cave :(

# Saving and Investment (continued)

2. **Investing in yourself is also important**. So invest in personal development and education.

3. **Investments should be diversified** – don't put all eggs in to one basket, because this minimized the risk.

4. **Start investing early** - as saying goes, the early bird catches the worm! The earlier you start saving and investing more money you will have (compounding return plays huge role in this).

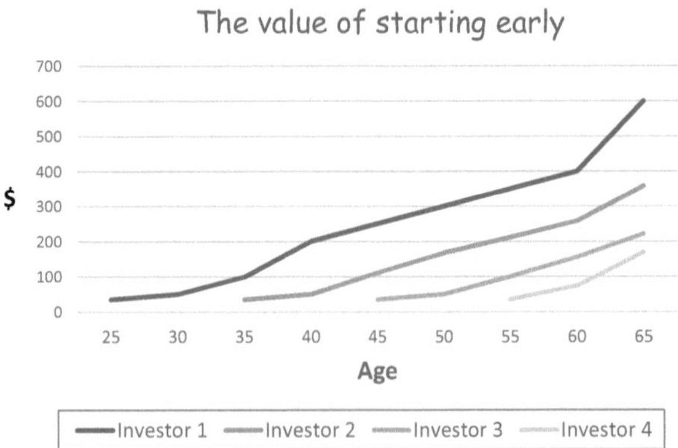

# Simple and Compounding interest

As we mentioned earlier, there are two types, **simple and compound.**

**Simple interest** is paid only on the sum of money that is first saved with the bank. If $10,000 is put in a bank account with an interest rate of 0.03 (3%), the amount will increase by the same figure each year or $300 per year <= ($10,000 * 0.03).

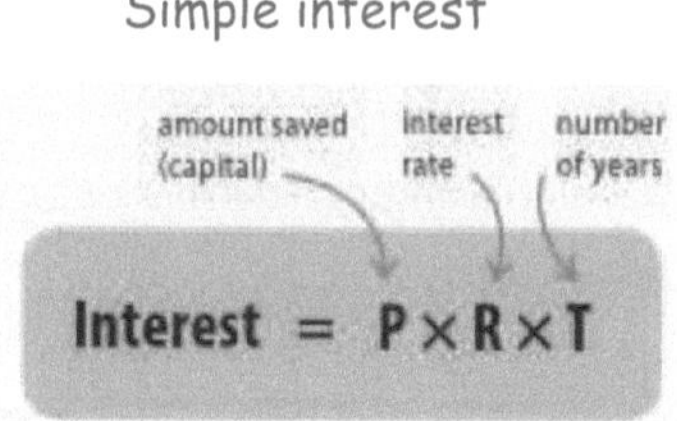


**Compound interest** is paid on the money invested <u>and any interest that is earned on that money.</u> If $10,000 is paid into a bank account with an interest rate of 0.03 (3%), then the amount will increase **because earned interest is reinvested.**

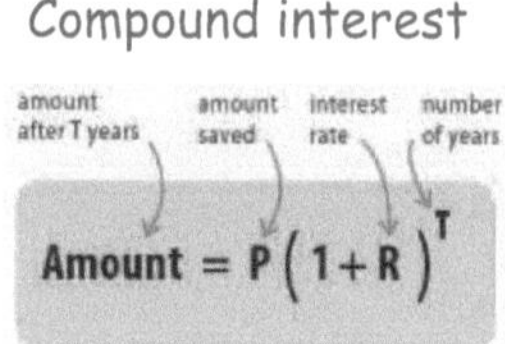

# Compounding

**Compounding** – is return on you reinvestments!
Savings is worth more, if principle and interest
income <u>are reinvested</u>.

Compound interest of 10% for 20 years (in Dinars)

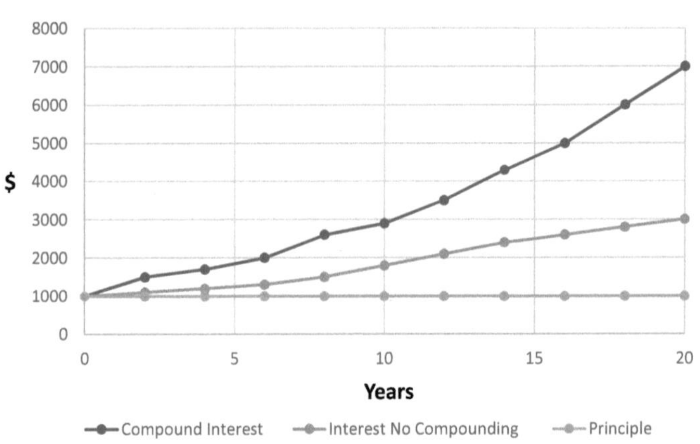

# Compounding (continued)

Compounding works only **if investment returns are not withdrawn and reinvested.** Compounding works better for longer term!

<u>Example of compounding at work:</u>

| Money (Dinars) | Annual rate (r) | Periods (y) | Compound (m) | Final amount (Dinars) | C-factor (final/initial) |
|---|---|---|---|---|---|
| 5,000.00 | 5% | 5 | 60 | 6,416.79 | 1 |
| 5,000.00 | 5% | 10 | 120 | 8,235.05 | 2 |
| 5,000.00 | 5% | 15 | 180 | 10,568.52 | 2 |
| 5,000.00 | 5% | 20 | 240 | 13,563.20 | 3 |
| 5,000.00 | 5% | 25 | 300 | 17,406.45 | 3 |
| 5,000.00 | 5% | 30 | 360 | 22,338.72 | 4 |
| 5,000.00 | 5% | 35 | 600 | 60,596.92 | 12 |
| 5,000.00 | 5% | 40 | 900 | 210,955.47 | 42 |

# The path for financial freedom

Keep in mind that the only constant thing in life is change! Life is full of surpises, so better be ready.

The benefit of financial freedom is peace of mind, without needing to borrow at a high interest rate or sell your belongings at a loss.

So, it is better not use your savings, hope for the best and get ready for the worst!

**Here are 4 steps for financial freedom:**

- Start saving early
- Have something for rainy days
- Lifestyle control
- Understand risks

# Start saving early

When your parents give you pocket money, **do not use it all in one go.** Put some of it into piggy bank and save it for later to buy something you really need.

If you get a bonus pocket money, put some of that to piggy bank as well.

Try to save on other things as well. **The point is to program the habit of saving into your life.**

Then, you will watch your money grow and this can be very motivating.

# Have something for rainy days

About 30% of American adults said they wouldn't have cash to cover an unexpected $400 expense (Fed survey, 2020). **Hence, start building emergency cash reserve before investing money elsewhere.**

You can use money from piggy bank too, but using them before it is full, requires breaking it earlier than planned.

Many financial wizards recommend **to have enough money that will see you through six months of expenses**, especially if your income comes from just one source.

The older you are and the higher your salary, the bigger your emergency fund should be, since it may take longer to find a job.

# Lifestyle control

Part of what makes it tough to have a rainy day stash is the need to save on everything.

As our piggy bank gets heavier and heavier, so will the temptation to spend without thinking: we want better toys, games and phones.

**So, don't let your spending rise with your income. Keep it under control!**

# Understand risks

Risk is probability of something going wrong or down.

For example, if you decided to use your piggy bank money to buy stocks and then prices go down. In this case **people often overestimate their ability to ride out drastic price movements (also called volatility).**

It is difficult to know beforehand if the game is worth the candle. The only way is to live through it and find it out for yourself.

# Alternative budget approach based on 50-30-20 plan!

**One-half (50%) of your pocket money or earnings should be spent on thins you really need.**

**We can call this a 'need' category, which includes,**

- All of your essential costs, such as food, books, clothes. Once you are adult things such as rent, mortgage payments, utilities, health insurance, debt payments and car payments may be added.

- If your 'need' expenses is more than half of your money, **you may have to cut some of it.**

# 20% of your money goes to piggy bank, it includes

- Putting money into a piggy bank, and once you grow up adding to retirement savings and any other investments, such as stocks, bonds, gold and etc.

- Putting money in your emergency fund to cover between three and six months worth of living expenses.

- While saving money, look for options with minimum cost such as (taxes, fees).

# 30% of your money goes toward things you want

**'want' category includes,**

- Games, toys, hamburgers, travel, shopping and basically fun.

- This category may also include upgrades: if you purchase a nicer bike instead of a less expensive one.

**Conclusion:** 50-30-20 plan may not be excellent, but it can be a good place to start if you're new to budgeting and are don't know hot to use your money wisely.

# Summary

Study well, work hard with a positive mental attitude. It is important to constantly learn and educate yourself about finance. In general, educated people make more money. For example,

Dino`s friend Lili earns 50 Dinars a month. She has graduated from school.

Dino`s brother Eric earns 70 Dinars a month. He has a  Bachelor`s degree.

Dino earns 90 Dinars because he has a Master`s degree and PhD.

Hi  kiddo,

Dino is happy you have been with him during this
reading journey. Remember some key advice –
get paid your worth, spend less than you earn
(stick to a budget), have a savings and always
remember to invest wisely!


Good luck and always remember Dino's advice for
financial success. The decisions we make now will
influence our future monetary habits.

You are dino-mite! Rawr!

# For Notes:

For Notes:

For Notes:

*Golib Kholjigitov was born in the beautiful city of Samarkand, which located on the ancient Silk Road, and was the epicenter of trade.*

*Golib is a finance expert and father of three budding young curious experts. He has received his Bachelor's degree in finance from Northern Arizona University and his Master's degree from Harvard University. He served as a Deputy minister of finance and currently teaches finance at the British Management University in Tashkent.*

*Golib believes it is never too early to introduce children to the wonderful world of finance!*

Written in Samarkand, Uzbekistan
Samarkand - 2021

ISBN    978-3-659-47045-5

Printed by Books on Demand GmbH, Norderstedt / Germany